Comfort

Comfort

RECIPES TO WARM THE HEART AND FEED THE SOUL

CAROLYN CALDICOTT

PHOTOGRAPHS BY CHRIS CALDICOTT
FOOD STYLING BY CAROLYN CALDICOTT

F
FRANCES LINCOLN LIMITED
PUBLISHERS

Frances Lincoln Limited
74–77 White Lion Street
London N1 9PF
www.franceslincoln.com

Comfort

Food styling by Carolyn Caldicott
Designed by Becky Clarke

First Frances Lincoln edition 2014

A catalogue record for this book is available from the British Library.

978-0-7112-3491-8

987654321

Contents

* * *

Introduction

★ ★ ★

*T*ired and hungry, got the blues or simply feel like spoiling yourself? Help is at hand. *Comfort* is packed full of hale and hearty, wholesome and warming, familiar favourites: food to pick you up, dust you down and put a spring back in your step.

Here are tasty and uncomplicated ideas for nutritious soothing suppers, lazy Sunday morning brunches, relaxed evenings with friends and indulgent treats – down-to-earth recipes that nurture the soul and leave you with a rosy glow.

So pull on a pair of woolly socks and a cosy jumper, turn up the volume on the radio and get cooking. Classic but with a contemporary twist, these recipes will surely put a smile back on your face.

Breakfasts worth getting up for

★ ★ ★

*T*he most important meal of the day, breakfast fortifies us for all the challenges that lie ahead, whether it's juggling a hectic schedule or making the most of a lazy Sunday with the papers. Maybe you need a nutritious quick fix, a luxurious brunch or perhaps the best hangover cure known to man after an evening on the tiles! You will find them all here . . .

Healthy or indulgent, never underestimate the comforting value of a good breakfast and remember to follow the wise advice of the famous saying to always 'breakfast like a king'.

HEALTHY AND HOMELY BREAKFASTS FOR A BUSY DAY

Breakfasts to tempt you from the cosy cocoon of the duvet and leave you feeling bright eyed, bushy tailed and ready to make the most of the day ahead.

PORRIDGE

A steaming bowl of creamy porridge is the perfect start to any day. As a complex carbohydrate it slowly releases energy to keep you going even through the hardest morning tasks, making it the ultimate super food breakfast.

If you want to keep things healthy stick to making your morning porridge with water and a teaspoon of linseed, serve topped with a splash of milk and honey, some goji berries and a sprinkling of pumpkin and sunflower seeds.

For something a little less virtuous simmer with equal quantities of milk and water and a good pinch of cinnamon, top with chopped banana and blueberries then drizzle on some maple syrup.

Weekends deserve to be more indulgent, so make it with just milk and stir a glug of double cream and a tot of whiskey into the thickened porridge then top with a knob of butter, brown sugar and another naughty dash of cream.

Rushing to get out the front door? Then rolled oats are the quickest option. Jumbo oats make a chunky textured porridge, but need a longer cooking time. Oatmeal or pinhead oats are the traditional choice, but it's best to first soak the oats over night in the measured quantity of liquid. Give the mixture a good stir in the morning, before cooking in the usual way overleaf.

Porridge provided the backbone to the Scottish crofters diet for centuries. A big pan of porridge would be prepared in the morning – always using oats, water and salt – and any leftovers were then poured into a special square wooden drawer. The cold set porridge was then cut into slices to make a nutritious pack lunch, or fried in butter for supper.

BASIC PORRIDGE RECIPE

For one person combine 1 teacup of oats with 2 teacups liquid (water or milk or a mixture of both), add a pinch of salt and bring to the boil stirring constantly. Reduce the heat to a minimum and gently simmer until the porridge thickens, the more you stir, the creamier the porridge becomes. So simple and so warming.

★ ★ ★

STRAWBERRY AND BLUEBERRY SMOOTHIE

Thick fruit smoothies are literally a meal in a glass; quick to prepare, they make a brilliant breakfast on the run. If time is just too tight, pour the smoothie into a travel cup and sip as you go.

FOR ONE GENEROUS SMOOTHIE
1 smallish banana
A handful of hulled strawberries
A handful of blueberries
A small wine glass of apple juice or milk
2 tablespoons natural yoghurt

Place all the ingredients in a blender and whiz until smooth.

HONEY TOASTED NUT AND SEED GRANOLA

Create your own self styled granola when you have the luxury of time on your hands and store in an air tight container ready for those mornings where time is of the essence. Just dollop with yoghurt, add a handful of chopped fruit, drizzle with runny honey and its ready to eat.

You can also use this recipe to mix your own luxury muesli; omit the honey, maple syrup and oil stage, and simply mix all the dry ingredients together untoasted.

3 tablespoons runny honey
3 tablespoons maple syrup
3 tablespoons sunflower oil
½ teaspoon ground cinnamon
½ teaspoon ground ginger
150g/5oz rolled oats
150g/5oz barley or spelt flakes
   or jumbo oats

150g/5oz mix of pumpkin, sesame,
   sunflower and linseed
175g/6oz mix of chopped almonds
   and walnuts
A handful of chopped dried apricots
A handful of chopped dried dates

Preheat the oven to 170°C/325°F/gas mark 3.

Warm the honey, maple syrup and oil in a small pan and whisk in the cinnamon and ginger.

Combine the remaining ingredients in a bowl (except for the dried fruit), pour the honey mixture over the top and gently mix together until all the ingredients are well coated.

Spread the granola on a large greaseproof baking tray and place in the oven for 20 minutes, turning the mixture a couple of times to ensure all the ingredients are evenly toasted.

Remove the granola from the oven and allow to cool completely before combining with the chopped dried fruit. Store the cooled granola in an airtight container.

FRUITY COMPOTE TOPPINGS

Luscious seasonal fruit compotes are perfect to spoon over porridge and granola. Strawberry and raspberry, blackcurrant and plum, blackberry and apple, rhubarb with a hint of ginger, look out for what's available in the market.

Gently simmer the prepared fruit with a splash of water and a touch of vanilla extract or cinnamon until soft, sweeten if necessary with brown sugar or honey to taste.

THE PERFECT SOFT-BOILED EGG AND SOLDIERS

Dipping buttery toasted soldiers into a soft-boiled egg is one of the greatest pleasures of life, and one that never dims with age. Forget all the jokes, there is a fine art to cooking a boiled egg; follow these basic rules and you will never be disappointed.

Always use the freshest possible free-range eggs stored at room temperature, if they are too cold they tend to crack when lowered into the hot water. To help avoid the egg cracking, puncture the blunt end of the egg with a pin.

Fill a small pan with enough water to just cover the eggs and bring the water to simmering point. Carefully lower the eggs into the simmering water, immediately check the time, and allow 4–5 minutes (depending on the eggs size, medium or large) for a soft-boiled egg and 5–6 minutes for a slightly firmer yolk.

After a minute or so toast your bread until golden brown and spread with generous quantities of butter. Cut the hot toast into finger-sized soldiers.

Remove the egg from the water and place in your favourite eggcup (remember to cut the top from the egg, otherwise it will continue to cook and ruin all your good work).

Sprinkle your perfectly cooked egg with sea salt and black pepper, or even a dash of Tabasco, and dip away.

HANGOVER BUSTING BREAKFAST

Pounding head, churning stomach? Nothing a good breakfast can't fix! A fry up is probably pushing it a bit too far, but potato rosti with poached egg, now you're talking comfort. What you need are simple recipes full of carb and protein to deliver a speedy recovery. If all else fails you can always resort to the hair of the dog and pour a stiff Bloody Mary!

BLOODY MARY

Forget coffee, caffeine dehydrates. On the other hand a Bloody Mary is bursting with vitamins and hydrating juice that delivers an instant shot of energy. Hopefully just enough to cook a slap up breakfast!

If you can't face more alcohol, skip the vodka and mix a Virgin Mary.

PER PERSON

Ice

Vodka, as little or as much as you desire

Juice of half a lemon

Tomato juice (to fill a high ball glass)

6 dashes of Worcester sauce

3 shakes of Tabasco

A sprinkle of back pepper and
  celery salt

A stick of celery

A thick slice of lemon

Half fill a high-ball glass with ice, pour in the vodka and lemon juice and top with tomato juice.

Add the Worcester sauce, Tabasco, black pepper and celery salt, stir everything together with the celery stick and float the sliced lemon on top.

QUICK FIX RELIEF

Believe it or not, bacon has been scientifically proven to help cure a hangover, not only is it full of protein, it is also high in amino acids that help clear the head. Fry a generous quantity of back bacon in olive oil and layer between slices of fresh bread with an obligatory squirt of brown sauce.

Bananas are chock a block with potassium and magnesium, both very useful minerals to help cure a hangover; team with protein and carb rich peanut butter topped toast and you have ticked all the boxes for an instant remedy, without even having to get a frying pan out.

POTATO ROSTI AND POACHED EGG

A lighter take on egg and chips, guaranteed to put you back on your feet. Why not go the whole hog and fry some fat sausages and tomatoes to go with it?

SERVES 4

3 medium sized waxy potatoes,
   peeled and medium grated
1 dessertspoon plain flour
Salt and black pepper

2 tablespoons olive oil
2 tablespoons of butter
Poached eggs (see page?)

Wrap the grated potato in a clean tea towel and squeeze away any excess water. Tip the potato into a bowl and combine with the flour and seasoning to taste.

Heat the olive oil and butter in a largish non-stick frying pan. When the butter starts to foam, add the potato and press down with the back of a spatula to compact into a rosti cake. Fry until brown and crunchy on both sides.

Cut into 4 and serve topped with poached eggs.

EGGY BREAD

Soft on the inside and crunchy on the outside, top eggy bread with crispy bacon or maple syrup for instant pain relief.

Cinnamon sugar is also delicious sprinkled onto eggy bread; mix 1 teaspoon ground cinnamon with 1 tablespoon golden caster sugar and sprinkle to taste.

PER PERSON
1 large free-range egg
1 generous tablespoon whole milk
A pinch of salt (and pepper if serving with bacon)
2 thick slices of good quality crusty white bread
A generous knob of butter

Streaky bacon grilled until crisp, maple syrup or cinnamon sugar to serve.

Whisk the egg and milk together until fluffy and season to taste. Place the bread in a shallow flat dish and coat both sides with the egg mixture. Leave to stand for a few minutes to allow the egg to soak into the bread.

Melt the butter in a non-stick frying pan, when the butter starts to foam, add the eggy bread and fry until golden brown on both sides. Serve immediately with your choice of topping.

LAZY MORNINGS

Hurray! No pressing obligations except to revel in the best leisurely breakfast imaginable. Take your time and try something a little more out of the ordinary, and having successfully completed your goal, indulge yourself in that wonderful guiltless pleasure of putting your feet up with the papers or a good book and dozing. Don't worry about the washing up, it can wait.

DEVILLED MUSHROOMS WITH CIABATTA TOAST

Chunky flat mushrooms oozing with spicy buttery devilled sauce, piled onto crunchy ciabatta toast.

SERVES 4
5 large flat mushrooms
60g/2½oz butter
1 small red onion, finely chopped
2 teaspoons Worcestershire sauce
A good shake of Tabasco or a large pinch of cayenne
2 teaspoons English mustard powder
4 generous tablespoons double cream
A good squeeze of lemon juice
Small handful of chopped curly parsley
Salt and black pepper
Toasted ciabatta to serve

Peel the mushrooms and cut into thick slices.

Melt the butter in a large frying pan, add the chopped onion and sauté together until golden brown. Add the mushrooms and continue to sauté until the mushrooms are nice and soft.

Whisk the Worcestershire sauce, Tabasco, double cream, mustard powder and lemon juice together. Gently combine the mixture with the mushrooms and cook together for a couple of minutes. Stir in the chopped parsley and season to taste.

Butter thick slices of ciabatta toast and pile the mushrooms on top.

SMOKED SALMON AND SCRAMBLED EGG MUFFINS WITH HERBY CRÈME FRAICHE

Scrambled egg and smoked salmon are simply made for each other. The secret to soft, melt in the mouth scrambled egg is to add a little double cream to the beaten eggs and to remove the pan from the heat before the egg looks completely cooked (the egg continues to cook until it is served).

SERVES 4
4 tablespoons full fat crème fraiche
1 dessertspoon chopped dill
Grated zest of ½ an unwaxed lemon
Salt and black pepper
6 large free-range eggs
A good splash of double cream
1 tablespoon chopped chives
Salt and black pepper
Butter
2 muffins
4 muffin sized slices smoked salmon

Whisk the crème fraiche with the dill and lemon zest and season to taste.

Beat the eggs with the double cream and stir in the chopped chives and seasoning to taste.

Heat a medium non-stick frying pan until really hot, add a large knob of butter and swirl it around the bottom of the pan until it has completely melted.

Pour in the beaten eggs, and as they start to set, stir constantly with a wooden spoon until the egg has a slightly runny scrambled egg texture. Remove the pan from the heat and prepare the muffins.

Quickly toast the split muffins, dollop the crème fraiche on top, cover with smoked salmon and pile the scrambled egg on top. Serve immediately.

PREFER TO POACH?

There is a knack to plump poached eggs with a soft centre; 2/3 fill a smallish pan with water, add a capful of white wine or cider vinegar and heat until simmering point is reached. Break a medium or large free-range egg onto a saucer and carefully slip the egg into the simmering water. Cook for 3–4 minutes for a runny yolk or 5–6 for a firmer centre. Lift the egg from the water with a slatted spoon and drain on a piece of kitchen paper before serving.

PLUMP PANCAKES

Pancakes put the fun back into breakfast time; serve rolled with honey and lemon juice, or maple syrup and mixed berries. If you prefer your pancakes savoury, fill with garlic mushrooms or melted cheese and bacon.

As the batter needs to stand for half an hour or so before making the pancakes, why not take the time to soak in a hot bath.

MAKES 12 PANCAKES
110g/4oz plain flour
2 large free-range eggs, beaten
275ml/½ pint whole milk
1 tablespoon sunflower oil, plus extra to fry
Pinch of salt

Sift the flour into a bowl and make a well in the middle.

Pour the beaten eggs into the well and combine with the flour. Gradually stir in the milk, taking care to crush any lumps as you do so. Add the salt and cover the bowl with cling film. Leave the batter to stand for ½ an hour.

Dip a sheet of kitchen paper into a little sunflower oil and wipe the oil across the bottom of a medium sized non-stick frying pan. Heat the frying pan until really hot, give the batter a quick stir, and ladle a serving spoon into the hot pan.

Swirl the batter around the bottom of the pan until it is completely coated. Cook the pancake for a couple of minutes until golden brown, run a spatula around the edge and carefully turn. Cook for a further few minutes until golden brown. If you are feeling brave why not try flipping the pancake?

Place the cooked pancakes in a warm oven until all the batter has been used up, then get rolling.

SMOKED HADDOCK KEDGEREE

This wonderful Indian inspired old-fashioned breakfast dish of smoked haddock, spiced rice and boiled egg is always a winner. If you are not keen on smoked fish, salmon fillets fried in butter make a good alternative.

SERVES 4
4 medium free-range eggs
2 teacups of basmati rice
450g/1lb undyed smoked haddock
2 bay leaves
½ teaspoon black peppercorns
3 good tablespoons of unsalted butter
1 large red onion, finely sliced
½ teaspoon ground coriander
½ teaspoon ground cumin
½ teaspoon ground turmeric
¼ teaspoon ground cardamom
Chilli flakes to taste
A handful of chopped coriander leaves or parsley if you prefer
Salt and black pepper
A large lemon cut into wedges

Boil the eggs for 10 minutes, remove from the pan and immerse immediately into a bowl of cold water until cool (this ensure the yolks stay a nice bright yellow). Peel the eggs and cut into chunks.

Wash the rice until the water runs clear, place in a saucepan along with 4 teacups of cold water. Bring the rice to the boil, then reduce the heat, cover the pan and gently simmer until the rice has absorbed all the water. Turn off the heat and allow the rice to sit for 5 minutes before fluffing with a fork.

Lay the smoked haddock in the bottom of a frying pan and cover with boiling water. Add the bay leaves and peppercorns and gently simmer together for 5 minutes.

Remove the fish from the pan and allow it to cool a little before flaking into bite size chunks (discarding the skin and any bones you come across).

Melt the butter in a large non-stick frying pan, add the chopped onion and sauté together until the onions are caramelised. Stir in the spices and cook for a minute or so before adding the cooked rice, stir-fry until the rice is evenly coated with the spice mixture and piping hot.

Gently combine the smoked haddock, hard-boiled egg and coriander with the rice over a low heat. Season the kedgeree to taste and served topped with the lemon wedges.

Hearty meals
for friends and family

★ ★ ★

We are talking about boisterous informal lunches and suppers here, not perfect dinner parties with manners to match. A chance to share good home cooked food with friends and family, fail safe familiar recipes that help you concentrate on the company and not the catering. Who can resist a deep filled pastry pie or a Sunday roast with all the trimmings?

PIE AND MASH

A proper deep filled homemade pie never fails to deliver a large slice of comfort; choose from crisp puff pastry or crunchy-topped creamy mash coveting a luscious steaming hot filling below.

Pies can be made well in advance of mealtimes and freeze brilliantly, leaving you with bags of time to join in with the hullabaloo of friends and family.

SHEPHERDS PIE

Topped with beautifully browned mashed potato, furrowed with a fork to resemble a ploughed field, shepherds pie is traditionally made with lamb mince or the leftovers from a lamb roast. Replace lamb with beef mince and shepherds pie miraculously transforms into a cottage pie.

Mashed sweet potato, celeriac or swede also work really well combined with the potato topping; simply reduce the quantity of potato by half and make up the difference with your choice of root vegetable.

If you are using the leftover meat from a lamb joint, brown the meat and simmer with half the listed amount of stock for half the amount of time then continue the recipe as normal.

SERVES 6

Olive oil

2 medium onions, diced

2 cloves crushed garlic

2 carrots, diced

2 parsnips, diced

750g/1½lb lamb mince
   or leftover diced lamb

1 tablespoon plain flour

2 tablespoon tomato puree

A good shake of Worcestershire sauce

425ml/¾ pint good stock (preferably lamb)

1 tablespoon chopped thyme

1 tablespoon chopped rosemary

2 bay leaves

Salt and black pepper

1 kilo/2lb 4oz mashing potatoes,
   peeled and cut into chunks

Milk

Butter

Nutmeg

Salt and black pepper

Heat a splash of olive oil in a large pan. When the oil is hot, add the onion and garlic and fry until soft. Add the carrot and parsnip and cook for a further 5 minutes or so until the vegetables start to soften.

Remove the vegetables from the pan, add an extra splash of olive oil and brown the meat in batches. Return the vegetables and meat to the pan and stir in the flour, tomato puree and a good shake of Worcestershire sauce.

Add the stock, thyme, rosemary, bay leaves and seasoning to taste. Give everything a good stir, cover the pan and gently simmer on the lowest heat for 30 minutes (stirring every once in a while to prevent sticking and adding extra stock if necessary to maintain a thick gravy).

Meanwhile cook the potatoes in simmering water until soft. Drain the potatoes well, return to the pan and steam dry over a low heat for a minute or so, shaking the pan constantly to prevent sticking. Add a splash of milk, a large knob of butter and good grate of nutmeg. Mash everything together until really smooth and season.

Preheat the oven to 190°C/375°F/Gas mark 5

To assemble the pie, remove the bay leaves and spoon the lamb into a large casserole or pie dish, cover with the mashed potato and draw furrows in the potato with the back of a fork.

Dot the potato liberally with butter, place on a baking tray, and bake in the preheated oven for 25–30 minutes until golden brown.

STEAK, KIDNEY AND PORCINI PIE

A rich meaty pie topped with thick puff pastry. Pile on a plate with creamy mashed potato and peas for a classic slice of comfort.

The pie filling conveniently improves with age, so can be put together the day before if you prefer. Bake in a large pie dish or alternatively it is rather nice to make little individual pies. Never feel guilty about topping your pie with pre-made pastry; no one will know it's not homemade!

SERVES 6

750g/1lb10oz cubed stewing steak
300g/11oz cubed lambs kidney
Salt and pepper
Olive oil
1 large onion, cubed
2 tablespoons plain flour
725ml/1¼ pint good beef stock

40g/1½oz dried porcini mushrooms
1 tablespoon hot horseradish
1 tablespoon mushroom ketchup
A small bunch of thyme
8 juniper berries
500g/1lb2oz puff pastry
1 small free-range egg, beaten

Season the steak and kidney, add a good glug of olive oil to a heavy bottomed pan, and brown the meat in batches.

Add the onions and fry for a further 5 minutes or so. Stir in the flour, and when well combined, pour in the stock.

Add the dried porcini, horseradish, mushroom ketchup, thyme and juniper berries, give the pan a good stir and bring to the boil.

Reduce the heat, cover the pan and gently simmer for 1½ hours, until the meat is tender and the gravy has thickened (stir the pan at regular intervals to prevent sticking and add extra stock if necessary to maintain a thick gravy).

Remove the thyme and spoon the filling into a large pie dish (or individual dishes). Set to one side and allow the filling to cool a little.

Preheat the oven to 200°C/400°F/Gas mark 6.

Roll out the puff pastry onto a floured surface. Brush the lip of the pie dish with beaten egg and carefully place the pastry on top. Trim away any excess pastry and firmly crimp the edges, brush with beaten egg and cut a small whole in the middle (to let the steam escape).

Place the pie on a baking tray and bake in the preheated oven for 30 minutes until the pastry is puffed up and golden.

CREAMY FISH PIE WITH A CHEESY POTATO TOPPING

Soft and soothing, a large fish pie is made for sharing. A couple of roughly chopped hard-boiled eggs, or a handful of sliced young leaf spinach can also make a good addition to the filling.

SERVES 6

900g/2lb mashing potatoes, peeled and cubed	8 black peppercorns
A splash of whole milk and double cream	500ml/18 floz whole milk
Butter	75g/3oz butter
Salt and black pepper	60g/2½oz plain flour
Grated mature Cheddar cheese to taste	1 tablespoon finely chopped dill
900g/2lb mixed fish fillets	Small handful curly parsley,
(including salmon, smoked haddock,	finely chopped
pollock or cod)	A good squeeze of lemon
150g/5oz large raw prawns	A good splash of double cream
2 bay leaves	Salt and black pepper

Cook the potatoes in boiling water until soft, drain well, return to the pan and steam dry over a low heat for a minute or so. Add a splash of milk and cream, a large knob of butter and seasoning to taste, mash together until really smooth.

Lay the fish fillets and prawns in a large frying pan, add the bay leaves and peppercorns and cover with 2/3 of the milk. Bring the pan to the boil, then reduce the heat and gently simmer for 5 minutes. Strain the milk from the pan into a jug, add the remaining milk, and set to one side ready to make the sauce.

Melt the butter in a small pan, stir in the plain flour and cook the resulting roux over a low heat for a few minutes. Remove the pan from the heat and gradually whisk in the strained milk mixture. Return the pan to the heat and gently cook together, stirring constantly, until the sauce coats the back of a wooden spoon. Add the chopped herbs, lemon juice, a good splash of cream and seasoning to taste.

Preheat the oven to 190°C/375°F/Gas mark 5.

Roughly break the fish into large chunks and place along with the prawns in the bottom of a large pie dish (removing any peppercorns or bay leaves). Pour the sauce evenly over the top and gently combine together. Cover the fish with the mashed potato and sprinkle with grated Cheddar cheese to taste.

Place the pie on a baking tray and bake in the preheated oven for 25–30 minutes, until golden brown.

ROAST CHICKEN
WITH ALL THE TRIMMINGS

The weekend wouldn't feel complete without a Sunday roast. Plump golden roast chicken, crunchy roast potatoes, caramelised root vegetables and creamy bread sauce – the ultimate ingredients for a long leisurely late lunch with all the gang.

HOW LONG TO ROAST?

A good rule of thumb is to roast the chicken for 20 minutes per 450g/1lb at 190°C/375°F/Gas mark 5, plus an extra 15 minutes. Increase the oven temperature to 220°C/425°F/Gas mark 6 for the last 10 minutes to ensure crispy brown skin.

PERFECT ROAST CHICKEN

Roast chicken is a blissfully uncomplicated dish to prepare, once it is in the oven there's not a great deal left to do, except sit back and relish the tantalising cooking aromas filling the kitchen.

It is essential to choose the best possible chicken you can afford and always try to stick to free-range.

For something more exotic smear the chicken with olive oil and a couple of heaped tablespoons of harissa paste and roast using the same method.

SERVES 6

1.6 kilo/3½lb chicken
1 lemon, cut in half lengthwise
4 garlic cloves
Handful of curly parsley
Small bunch of thyme

50g/2oz soft butter
Salt and black pepper
1 medium red onion, peeled and
   cut into quarters

Preheat the oven to 190°C/375°F/Gas mark 6.

Stuff the chicken's cavity with the lemon, garlic, parsley and thyme. Smear the skin with butter and sprinkle generously with salt and black pepper.

Place the onion chunks in the middle of a roasting pan and pop the prepared chicken on top (the onion stops the chicken sitting in fat and adds extra flavour to the gravy).

Cover the chicken with kitchen foil and place in the preheated oven for 1¼ hour (remove the foil after 30 minutes and baste the chicken. Baste for a second time after a further 30 minutes). After 1¼ hour increase the oven temperature to 220°C/425°F/gas mark 6 and cook for a further 10–15 minutes until the skin is nice and brown.

To check the chicken is cooked through, insert a skewer into the thickest part of the leg – the escaping juices should run clear with no visible pinkish colour.

Remove the chicken from the pan, place on a warmed plate, cover with kitchen foil and a clean tea towel and allow to rest for 15 minutes before carving.

Keep the juices and the onion left in the roasting tin to make the gravy.

PERFECT ROAST POTATOES

Roast potatoes couldn't be simpler. For the best results, first parboil the prepared potato chunks for 10 minutes in simmering water. Drain the potatoes, return to the pan and steam dry for a minute or so over a low heat, shaking the pan as you do so.

The parboiled potatoes need about an hour to cook. Place in the oven when the chicken has 1 hour left of cooking time; the increased oven temperature at the end finishes the roast potatoes off perfectly. If you prefer your potatoes really brown, leave them in the oven for a little longer while you prepare the gravy.

Duck fat makes all the difference to a crunchy roast potato, but olive oil is a lighter option. Whichever you choose, it is essential to heat the oil first in a roasting tin in the oven for 5 minutes until really hot. Toss the parboiled potatoes in the hot oil until well coated, return the roasting tin to the oven and roast for a full hour, turning the potatoes a couple of times to prevent the potatoes from sticking and to ensure they are brown on all sides.

For 6 hungry people allow around 1.35 kilo/3lbs of roasting potatoes. Peel and cut the potatoes into equal sized large chunks, if the potatoes are small leave them whole. For this quantity of potatoes you will need 4 good tablespoons of duck fat or olive oil.

Season your perfectly roasted potatoes with salt to taste just before serving.

BALSAMIC, BUTTER AND THYME
ROAST PARSNIP AND CARROTS

No fuss roast parsnips and carrots make light work of vegetables to accompany a roast. If you love garlic add a whole head cut in half across the middle. Add the prepared vegetables to the oven when the chicken has 30 minutes left to cook, and leave them in to brown while the chicken is resting.

SERVES 6
4 medium parsnips, peeled and cut into finger sized pieces
3 medium carrots, peeled and quartered lengthwise
3 tablespoons butter
1 tablespoons olive oil
1½ tablespoons balsamic vinegar
1 generous tablespoon runny honey
Salt and freshly ground black pepper
1 dessertspoon chopped fresh thyme

Parboil the prepared parsnips and carrots for 5 minutes, drain well and dry completely in a clean tea towel.

Place the butter, olive oil, balsamic vinegar and honey in a small pan and gently warm together until the butter has melted.

Place the vegetables in a roasting pan, pour the sauce evenly over the top and turn them in the sauce until evenly coated. Arrange the vegetables in a single layer and season to taste.

Place the pan in the preheated oven, along with the chicken, 30 minutes before the end of the calculated cooking time. Leave the vegetables to caramelise in the oven while the meat is resting, then reduce the oven to a minimum until ready to serve. Just before serving sprinkle the parsnips with the chopped thyme.

HOMEMADE GRAVY

Homemade gravy completes a traditional roast – don't skimp, you can never have too much – and any leftovers can be used to make soup the next day.

1 tablespoon plain flour
A splash of wine (whatever you have open)
750ml/1¼ pint hot chicken stock
Salt and black pepper

Retrieve your roasting pan, complete with oniony bits and chicken juices. Every chicken is different, some are fattier than others, if there seems to be a lot of fat left in the roasting tin, tip some off.

Mix the plain flour with a little cold water in a medium bowl (just enough to make a thin paste), whisk in the hot stock.

Place the roasting tin over a medium heat on the stovetop. When the juices start to bubble, add a splash of wine and stir well, scraping any crusty bits from the tin as you do so.

Pour the stock into the pan and gently simmer, stirring constantly, until the gravy thickens (you don't want the gravy to be too thick). Pour the gravy into a warm gravy boat or jug and serve immediately.

CREAMY BREAD SAUCE

A superb clove spiced traditional sauce inseparable from roast chicken. Prepare the sauce when the chicken goes in the oven to allow the flavours to infuse.

1 medium onion, peeled and cut in half
8 cloves
2 bay leaves
8 peppercorns
425ml/¾ pint whole milk
85g/3½oz crust less day old good white bread
A large knob of butter
A splash of double cream
Freshly grated nutmeg
Salt

Stud the onion halves with the cloves and place in a saucepan along with the milk, bay leaves and peppercorns. Gently simmer over a low heat for 10 minutes.

Meanwhile dice the bread and whiz in a food processor until breadcrumbs form.

Add the breadcrumbs to the pan and simmer until the breadcrumbs absorb the milk to make a thickish sauce.

Remove the pan from the heat and allow the flavours to combine while the chicken is cooking.

Just before the roast is ready to serve, remove the onion and bay leaves, add the butter and a splash of double cream (enough to loosen the sauce) and gently warm together until the butter has melted.

Stir in a generous grate of nutmeg and season to taste.

CLASSIC CROWD PLEASERS

Hearty, no fuss cooking at its best. Cheap and cheerful crowd pleasers that are guaranteed to raise the volume.

TOAD IN THE HOLE

Yorkshire pudding and plump sausages smothered in onion gravy. Need I say more?

SERVES 6
175g/6oz plain flour
3 medium free-range eggs
425ml/¾ pint skimmed milk
1 heaped dessertspoon grainy mustard
8 slices of streaky bacon
8 good quality fat sausages
1 tablespoon olive oil
Salt and black pepper

Preheat the oven to 220°C/425°F/Gas mark 7.

First prepare the batter, sift the flour into a bowl and make a well in the centre. Beat the eggs with the milk and mustard until light and fluffy. Gradually pour the mixture into the well, stirring constantly until a smooth batter forms. Season the batter to taste.

Cut the rind from the bacon, stretch a little and wrap one slice around each sausage. Place the sausages in a roasting tin and drizzle with the olive oil, cook in the preheated oven for 10 minutes, turning the sausages after 5 minutes.

Give the batter a quick stir, evenly space the sausages in the roasting tin and pour the batter around them (it is important that the tin is really hot at this stage to create the best puffy Yorkshire pudding).

Return the tin to the oven and cook for a further 30 minutes, until the Yorkshire pudding is brown on top and puffed up. Cut into portions and serve with onion gravy (see page 62).

CHICKEN AND MANGO COCONUT CURRY

A large pot of curry is warming in more ways than one, and tastes even better when made the day before. Cook up a large pan of basmati rice to go with it, and place everything in the middle of the table, pans and all. Add a pile of popadoms and a bowl of seasoned yoghurt mixed with diced cucumber and dig in.

SERVES 6
4 large chicken breasts
Sunflower oil
1 large onion, diced
3 garlic cloves, crushed
A thumb sized piece of ginger root,
    peeled and grated
Sliced red chilli to taste
1 heaped teaspoon ground coriander
1 heaped teaspoon ground cumin
½ teaspoon turmeric

½ teaspoon cracked black pepper
4 crushed cardamom pods
1 large mango, peeled and cubed
570ml/1 pint coconut milk
4 tablespoons double cream
1 teaspoon garam masala
Salt
A handful of chopped coriander
    leaves to serve

Cut the chicken breasts into strips and season with salt. Add a good splash of sunflower oil to a heavy bottomed pan and brown the chicken in batches.

Remove the chicken from the pan and set to one side. Add the onion, garlic, ginger and chilli (and extra oil if necessary) and stir-fry until soft.

Combine the spices and stir into the onion mixture, cook for a couple of minutes, then return the chicken to the pan.

Add the mango, coconut milk and a splash of water and give everything a good stir. Bring the curry to simmering point (taking care to never allow the coconut milk to boil) and gently cook for 15 minutes until the sauce thickens and the chicken is cooked through.

Stir in the cream and the garam masala and season the curry to taste, sprinkle with chopped coriander leaves just before serving.

PUTTANESCA PASTA WITH A TWIST

Puttanesca pasta packs a punch; full of salty, spicy flavours, it makes a speedy store cupboard recipe to rustle up for an impromptu get together. Serve steaming hot topped with grated Parmesan.

SERVES 6

Olive oil
1 medium red onion, diced
4 cloves garlic, crushed
2 small red chillies
½ teaspoon chilli flakes
1 red pepper, thinly sliced
8 salted anchovy fillet,
   rinsed and dried
2 x 400g/14oz tins chopped
   plum tomatoes

2 heaped tablespoons salted capers,
   rinsed and dried
6 sun-dried tomatoes, sliced
A handful of pitted black olives,
   roughly chopped
A handful of chopped basil and oregano
Salt and pepper to taste
500g/1lb 4oz spaghetti
Olive oil
Grated Parmesan to serve

Add a good glug of olive oil to a heavy bottomed saucepan and fry the onion, garlic, chilli and pepper until soft.

Add the anchovies, roughly breaking them up with the back of a wooden spoon. Add the tomatoes, capers, sun-dried tomatoes, chopped olives and herbs.

Give everything a good stir, cover the pan and gently simmer until the sauce has thickened to a rich and oily texture. Season to taste (remembering the sauce will already be quite salty).

Cook the spaghetti in a large pan of salted boiling water until al dente, drain and toss with a drizzle of olive oil. Serve the spaghetti covered with the puttanesca sauce and topped with a liberal sprinkling of grated Parmesan.

Simple suppers

★ ★ ★

*S*imple satisfying suppers to hole up and wind down with are definitely called for after a hectic day. Whether you are home alone or spending a quiet evening in the company of a good friend, this chapter offers real meals to potter about the kitchen with and tempting recipes to shake away the day, leaving you with that 'there's no place like home' feeling.

BACK TO BASICS

Classic comfort food recipes for feel good suppers to enjoy on cosy evenings at home.

HOMEMADE BEEF BURGERS WITH MELTED MOZZARELLA, BEETROOT AND HORSERADISH MAYO AND SWEET POTATO CHIPS

Fabulous fast food at its best.

SERVES 4

450g/1lb beef steak mince
1 small red onion, minced
2 tablespoon salted capers,
   rinsed, dried and roughly chopped
2 teaspoons chopped rosemary
2 medium free-range egg yolks
Salt and black pepper
Sunflower oil
4 thick slices mozzarella cheese

1 medium sized cooked beetroot
   (without vinegar), grated
I gherkin, finely chopped
1 heaped teaspoon hot horseradish
4 generous tablespoons mayonnaise
Salt and black pepper
1 large sweet potato
4 tablespoons sunflower oil
Paprika to dust
4 crusty rolls, cut in half

Combine the beef mince with the onions, capers and rosemary, stir in the egg yolk and season to taste. Divide the mixture in half, roll each half into a ball and flatten to make a thickish burger. Drizzle both sides of the burgers with a little sunflower oil and set to one side.

Mix the grated beetroot with the chopped gherkin, horseradish and mayonnaise; season the mixture to taste.

Peel the sweet potato and cut into fattish chips. Heat the oil in a frying pan and fry the sweet potato chips in two batches, until golden brown on the outside and soft on the inside. Dust the chips with a sprinkling of paprika and keep warm while you cook the burgers.

Heat a heavy bottomed frying pan or griddle until it is really hot, add the burgers and fry for 4–5 minutes. Flip the burgers and pop the mozzarella on top, cook for a further 4–5 minutes, until the mozzarella has softened and the burger is brown on the outside but still a little pink in the middle (if you prefer your burgers medium, cook for 6–7 minutes on each side). Remove the burgers and warm the cut sides of the bun in the pan for a couple of minutes (the buns will soak up all the lovely juices).

To assemble the burgers, spread the beetroot mayo on the bottom half of the roll, place the burger on top, and cover with the roll lid. Serve immediately with the sweet potato chips.

SAUSAGES, LEEK MASH AND ONION GRAVY

Good old sausages and mash – suppers don't get more comforting than this.
For an extra special touch top the sausages and mash with wafer thin slices of parsnip fried in olive oil until crisp.

SERVES 4
8 good quality fat sausages
Olive oil

The leek mash
900g/2lb mashing potatoes,
    peeled and cut into chunks
2 medium sized leeks,
    cleaned and thinly sliced
110g/4oz butter
A good splash of milk
Salt and freshly ground black pepper

The red onion gravy
1 tablespoon olive oil
1 heaped tablespoon butter
1 large onion, thinly sliced
2 cloves garlic, crushed
A couple of sprigs of thyme
Splash of red wine or balsamic vinegar
425ml/¾ pint vegetable stock
A rounded teaspoon plain flour
    dissolved in a little water to
    make a thin paste
1 heaped tablespoon grainy mustard
Salt and black pepper

Simmer the potatoes in salted water until they feel soft when inserted with the point of a knife. Drain the potatoes, return to the pan and heat for a minute or so over a lowish temperature to dry any excess water.
While the potatoes are cooking, sauté the leeks in a ⅓ of the quantity of butter, until they are soft but not brown, remove from the pan and set to one side.
Add the remaining butter and a good splash of milk to the cooked potatoes and mash together until really smooth with no visible lumps. Beat the mash with a wooden spoon until creamy then fold in the sautéed leeks and seasoning to taste.
To make the gravy heat the olive oil and butter in a frying pan, when the butter starts to foam add the onion, garlic and thyme. Cover the pan and cook on a lowish heat until the onions are really soft and caramelised. Turn up the heat and add a

splash of red wine or balsamic vinegar, cook together until the liquid has reduced. Pour in the stock and the flour water, give everything a good stir, then reduce the heat and gently simmer until the gravy has thickened. Stir in the mustard and adjust the seasoning to taste.

Prick the sausages and fry in a little olive oil until they are nice and brown on the outside and cooked through.

Give the mashed potato and gravy a burst of heat before plating up.

CAULIFLOWER CHEESE

Never underestimate this cheap and cheerful cheesy childhood classic. Top with crispy fried streaky bacon and whole flat mushrooms fried in butter to make it even better.

SERVES 4
1 medium cauliflower
40g/1½oz butter
40g/1½oz plain flour
425ml/¾ pint whole milk
125g/4½oz strong Cheddar cheese, grated
1 teaspoon English mustard
Pinch of cayenne pepper
Salt and black pepper
20g/¾oz grated Parmesan cheese
Crispy fried streaky bacon and flat mushrooms fried in butter to serve

Preheat the oven to 200°C/400°F/Gas mark 6.

Cut the cauliflower into largish florets and simmer in salted water until just soft. Drain the cauliflower, and to ensure it is really dry, leave it draining in the colander over the pan while you prepare the sauce.

Melt the butter in a saucepan, stir in the flour and cook the resulting roux for a minute or so. Remove the pan from the heat and whisk in the milk. Return the pan to the heat and gently cook, stirring constantly, until the sauce thickens. Add ¾ of the grated cheddar and stir together until the cheese has melted. Add the mustard, cayenne and seasoning to taste.

Place the cauliflower in a heatproof dish and pour the sauce evenly over the top. Sprinkle the cauliflower with the remaining Cheddar and Parmesan cheese.

Place on a baking tray and bake in the preheated oven for 25 minutes, until golden brown.

UNDER THE WEATHER?

Recipes for those 'out of sorts' moments, when your body is crying out for something light and nutritious and easy to eat.

CINNAMON SPICED BUTTERNUT SQUASH SOUP WITH CHEESY CROUTON TOPPING

Tucking into a steaming bowl of hot soup is like a warm hug on a chilly day.

And best of all you can store it in portions in the freezer for when you need it most.

MAKES 6 PORTIONS

4 tablespoons sunflower oil
I medium onion, roughly chopped
2 cloves garlic, crushed
1 thumb sized piece of ginger
   root peeled and grated

1 medium butternut squash,
   peeled, deseeded and diced
1 medium potato, peeled and diced
1 teaspoon ground cinnamon
1.2 litre/2 pints good vegetable stock
Salt and black pepper

Cheesy crouton topping (per person)
1 thickish slice day old baguette
Butter
Grated Gruyere cheese

Heat the sunflower oil in a large saucepan, add the onion, garlic and ginger and fry until soft.

Add the butternut squash and potato, cover the pan and sweat the vegetables together until they start to soften (stir the pan every once in a while to prevent the vegetables sticking).

Stir in the cinnamon and add the stock. Bring the soup to the boil, then reduce the heat, cover the pan and gently simmer until the vegetables are soft.

Blend the soup until smooth and season to taste.

Butter both sides of the sliced baguette, place in a hot pan and fry until golden and crunchy. Flip the baguette and top with the grated Gruyere cheese, cook for a further few minutes until the cheese has melted.

Ladle the soup into a deep bowl and carefully float the crouton on top.

EGGS BAKED IN CREAM WITH ASPARAGUS SPEARS AND TOASTED SOLDIERS

Little pots of goodness to tempt the appetite. Dip lightly cooked asparagus spears and crunchy toasted soldiers into the runny yolk.

For something more substantial pop a serving of well-drained wilted spinach in the bottom of each ramekin and if your appetite is good, why not have two?

PER RAMEKIN POT
Butter
1 large free-range egg
1 tablespoon double cream
Freshly grated nutmeg
Salt and black pepper

To serve
A small handful of asparagus spears
Buttered toast cut into finger-sized soldiers

Preheat the oven to 190°C/375°F/Gas mark 5

Grease the inside of the ramekin with a generous amount of butter. Carefully break the egg into the ramekin and spoon in the cream. Grate nutmeg on top and season with salt and black pepper to taste.

Place the ramekin on a baking sheet and bake for 10 minutes in the preheated oven, until the white is cooked through, the yolk is still soft and the cream is bubbling hot.

While the eggs are baking in the oven, cook the asparagus spears in salted simmering water until al dente and prepare the soldiers, serve while still hot with the baked eggs.

PROPER FISH FINGER SANDWICHES

Chunky homemade fish fingers, sandwiched with dill mayonnaise and watercress between slices of fresh bread, make a powerful antidote to that lack lustre feeling.

SERVES 2
50g/2oz crustless day old bread
275g/10oz chunky white skinless fish fillets, such as polack or cod
Salt and black pepper
2 tablespoons plain flour
1 medium free-range egg, beaten
1 heaped tablespoon butter
2 generous tablespoons mayonnaise
1 teaspoon finely chopped curly parsley
A good squeeze of lemon juice
Salt and black pepper
4 slices buttered crusty bread
A handful of watercress

Break the bread into small chunks and whiz in a processor until breadcrumbs form.

Cut the fish into 6 largish fish finger shaped portions (removing any bones you come across) and season to taste.

Coat the fish with flour, dip in the beaten egg and cover with breadcrumbs.

Heat the butter in a frying pan and when the butter starts to foam, add the fish fingers and fry until golden brown on all sides.

Combine the mayonnaise with the dill and lemon juice and season to taste.

Spread 2 slices of buttered bread with dill mayonnaise, top with the fish fingers and watercress and cover with the remaining bread. Cut the sandwiches in half and serve immediately.

SIMPLY SPECIAL

Instant wow factor suppers with the minimum of effort. Recipes that inspire the imagination when you don't feel like going out, but fancy something a little bit special.

LEMON SOLE IN CAPER BUTTER

Buttery, succulent sole with capers makes a restaurant worthy supper in seconds. Serve with new potatoes and wilted baby spinach.

SERVES 2
2 Lemon sole fillets
Salt and black pepper
Plain flour
2 dessertspoons olive oil
2 generous tablespoons butter
2 tablespoons salted capers, rinsed and dried
A dessertspoon finely chopped flat leaf parsley
A good squeeze of lemon

Season the fish and dust with a little plain flour.

Heat the olive oil in a large frying pan, add the sole and fry for a few minutes on both sides until golden brown on the outside and cooked through. Remove the fish from the pan and place on a heated plate.

Add the butter to the pan and when it starts to foam add the capers, flat leaf parsley and a good squeeze of lemon. Cook for a minute or so, then return the sole to the pan, spoon the sauce over the fish and serve immediately.

CHUNKY SALMON FISHCAKES WITH CHIVE CREAM

Flaked salmon chunks and mashed potato are a marriage made in heaven – add a pool of chive cream and it just keeps getting better.

SERVES 2

200g/7oz mashing potatoes, peeled and cubed	Salt and black pepper
200g/7oz cooked salmon fillets	Plain flour to coat the fishcakes
2 tablespoons butter	Butter to fry
3 spring onions, thinly sliced	1 plump garlic clove, crushed
1 heaped tablespoon caper berries, stalks removed and roughly chopped	100ml/4floz single cream
1 tablespoon finely chopped dill	1 dessertpoon chopped chives
Grated zest of a lemon	A good squeeze of lemon juice
1 small free-range egg, beaten	Salt and black pepper
	Wilted spinach to serve

Cook the potatoes in salted water until soft, drain well, return to the pan and steam dry over a low heat for a couple of minutes (shaking the pan constantly to prevent the potatoes sticking). Roughly mash the potato until it is still quite lumpy. Set to one side and allow to cool. Break the fish into chunks, discarding any skin or bones.

Melt the butter in a small pan and soften the spring onions.

Gently combine the mashed potato, fish chunks, softened spring onion, chopped caper berries, parsley, lemon zest and beaten egg. Season the mixture to taste and shape into 8 plump fishcakes. Lightly coat the fishcakes with plain flour.

To make the chive cream, add the garlic to the same pan in which the spring onions were softened, add a small knob of butter and cook until soft and golden. Stir in the cream and the chopped chives and gently simmer for a couple of minutes. Add a good squeeze of lemon juice and seasoning to taste and cook for a further few minutes, until the cream has thickened slightly.

Melt a large knob of butter in a frying pan and fry the fish cakes in batches until golden brown on both sides, adding extra butter when necessary. Pop 2 fishcakes on each plate and spoon the chive cream around the edge.

WHOLE CAMEMBERT BAKED WITH GARLIC AND ROSEMARY

Hot molten Camembert makes a sublime supper for two. Warm a baguette and cut a few crudités, break the skin and dip. Serve with chutney, green salad and mixed charcuterie.

SERVES 2
1 whole room temperature Camembert (250g/9oz size in a wooden box)
1 plump clove of garlic, sliced
1 sprig of rosemary

To serve
Warm baguette or ciabatta
Mixed crudités – carrot, celery, raw mushrooms, fennel, apple....
Chutney
Green salad
Slices of your favourite saucisson and ham

Preheat the oven to 190°C/375°F/gas mark 5
    Tip the Camembert out of its wooden box, remove the wrapping and carefully squeeze the cheese back into the box. Using a small knife make a few slits in the top of the cheese and insert the garlic slices and rosemary leaves.
    Place the Camembert on a baking tray and bake in the preheated oven for 15 minutes or so, until the garlic is golden, the cheese has a slightly swollen appearance and feels soft and molten to the touch.

ROSEMARY AND ANCHOVY BARNSLEY CHOPS

Double sized lamb chops smeared with anchovy, rosemary and garlic make a unique old-fashioned taste sensation. Serve with mashed potato and green beans.

SERVES 2
2 salted anchovies, rinsed and dried
2 garlic cloves, crushed
2 sprigs rosemary, leaves removed and
     finely chopped
1 tablespoon olive oil
Black pepper
2 Barnsley chops (or 4 lamb chops)

Combine the anchovies with the crushed garlic and chopped rosemary and stir together until the anchovies break down. Add the olive oil and black pepper to taste. Smear the Barnsley chops with the mixture and leave to marinade for 30 minutes or so.

Heat a heavy bottomed frying pan and fry the chops for 5 minutes on each side until brown on the outside and pink in the middle (if you prefer your meat medium, fry for 7–8 minutes).

Perfect puddings

★ ★ ★

'*Naughty but nice.*' Who can resist a toe curlingly good pudding? There is something deeply comforting about pudding. Thick custard, sweet spongy treacle pudding, we all have our favourites, age old family recipes, some with more than a hint of the nursery about them. A slap up meal is simply incomplete without a pudding, so forget about the waistline and get stuck in.

All pudding recipes serve 4–6; depending on how greedy you are feeling!

RUM AND RAISIN BREAD AND BUTTER PUDDING

Who would have thought day old bread could taste so good? Try making with sliced croissant or panettone for a decadent twist.

50g/2oz golden raisins
3 tablespoons rum
  (preferably spiced rum)
425ml/¾ pint whole milk
1 slit vanilla pod
Soft butter

8 slices of day old white bread
  cut from a medium loaf
3 large free-range eggs
40g/1½oz caster sugar
75ml/¼ pint double cream
Freshly grated nutmeg and
  Demerara sugar to taste

Soak the raisins in the rum while you prepare the rest of the pudding.

Warm the milk with the vanilla pod, removing the pan from the heat just before boiling point is reached. Set to one side and allow the vanilla to infuse with the milk.

Generously butter the bread slices and cut diagonally into triangle shapes. Butter a medium sized deep heat-proof dish; lay half the bread in the bottom of the dish, overlapping the slices as you do so.

To make the custard, beat the eggs and sugar together in a medium sized bowl until light and fluffy. Remove the vanilla pod from the warm milk and whisk the infused milk into the egg mixture. Finally stir in the cream.

Pour half the custard mixture evenly over the bread lining the dish, scatter with the rum and raisins and layer the remaining bread on top. Pour the last of the custard over the bread and sprinkle with grated nutmeg and Demerara sugar to taste.

Dot the top of the pudding with a little extra butter and allow the custard to soak into the bread while the oven heats up.

Heat the oven to 180°C/350°F/Gas mark 4 and bake the pudding for 30–35 minutes until brown and caramelised on top.

CLOTTED CREAM RICE PUDDING

Forget school dinners, rich unctuous clotted cream makes this humble pudding shine. Top with an obligatory dollop of homemade jam as a homage to school days past.

If you are already using the oven for the main course, slip a rice pudding in the bottom of the oven and leave it to bubble away.

Butter
1 litre/1¾ pint Jersey or whole milk
50g/2oz golden caster sugar
1 vanilla pod slit lengthwise
110g/4oz short grain pudding rice
6 generous tablespoons clotted cream
Freshly grated nutmeg
Jam to serve

Preheat the oven to 150°C/300°F/Gas mark 2, or alternatively, if you are already using the oven at a higher temperature, place the pudding in the bottom of the oven and bake for ½ hour less cooking time, the pudding is ready when a golden brown skin has formed and it has a slight wobble when given a gentle shake.

Grease a medium sized ovenproof dish with butter.

Pour the milk into a saucepan, add the caster sugar and the seeds scraped from the inside of the slit vanilla pod and stir together over a low heat until the sugar has dissolved.

Add the rice and bring to the boil, reduce the heat and simmer for a few minutes until the rice starts to swell. Stir in the clotted cream and when the cream has completely melted, pour the mixture into the prepared ovenproof dish. Dot the top of the pudding with a little extra butter and grate a generous amount of nutmeg on top.

Cook the pudding in the preheated oven for 1½ hour, until the top is golden brown and the rice is soft.

STRAWBERRY AND PORT TRIFLE

A spectacular old fashioned trifle without a drop of jelly in sight.

Using ready-made custard makes this a show stopper pud with the minimum of effort.

Leftover Victoria sponge makes perfect trifle sponge or alternatively ready made trifle sponges are easily available – pick up a tub of shop bought custard at the same time, just make sure it is the thick kind.

450g/1lb strawberries
2 tablespoons caster sugar
5 tablespoons port
1 teaspoon vanilla extract
6 trifle sponges
570ml/1 pint ready made thick custard
300ml/½ pint double cream
A handful of toasted flaked almonds

Hull the strawberries and cut them in half; set a few to one side to decorate the top of the trifle.

Combine the caster sugar with the port and a dash of water in a saucepan. Warm together over a low heat until the sugar melts and the liquid is syrupy. Add the strawberries and vanilla extract and gently poach for a further couple of minutes until the fruit starts to soften.

Lay the trifle sponges in the bottom of a glass dish and spoon the strawberry mixture evenly over the top, cover with the custard and chill in the fridge for 1 hour.

Just before serving whip the cream until it forms soft peaks and dollop over the custard. Decorate the trifle with the toasted flaked almonds and the remaining strawberries.

STEAMED SYRUP AND HONEY PUDDING

Steamed syrup pudding is simply the last word in comforting puds – light fluffy sponge infused with warm syrup, best served smothered with homemade custard.

2 tablespoons golden syrup mixed with 2 tablespoon runny honey,
    plus extra to serve
175g/6oz soft butter, cubed (plus extra to grease the basin)
150g/5oz golden caster sugar
2 large free-range eggs
1 teaspoon vanilla extract
175g/6oz self raising flour

You will also need tinfoil, greaseproof paper and string.

Cut a piece of tinfoil and greaseproof paper large enough to cover your pudding dish.

Generously grease a medium sized ovenproof pudding basin with butter and spoon the syrup honey mixture in the bottom.

Cream the butter and caster sugar together until light and fluffy. Beat in the eggs one by one and stir in the vanilla essence. Fold in the flour and spoon the mixture into the basin.

Lay the tinfoil on top of the greaseproof paper and make a pleat down the middle, cover the pudding and secure with a length of string. Use an extra piece of string to make a handle.

Place the pudding in a saucepan and pour enough boiling water into the pan to reach approximately 7.5cm/3 inches up the side of the basin. Cover the pan and simmer for 1 hour 50 minutes, topping up with water if necessary.

Warm 1 tablespoon of golden syrup with 1 tablespoon honey. Run a palate knife around the edge of the pudding to help loosen it from the bowl, and turn out onto a plate. Pour the warm syrup over the pudding and serve whilst piping hot.

Snack attack

★ ★ ★

*H*aving a midnight munchy moment, feeling in need of a pick me up, or just craving a comforting snack? Take your pick from these snack attack specials.

SUN-DRIED TOMATO HUMMUS AND CRUDITÉS

Hummus always hits the spot – it's nutritious and full of flavour. Serve with vegetable crudités and warm pitta bread.

SERVES 4

1 x 400g/14oz tin chickpeas
4 sun-dried tomatoes in olive oil
1 plump clove garlic
Juice of a small lemon

2 tablespoons light tahini
3 tablespoons olive oil
Salt and black pepper to taste

Drain and rinse the chickpeas and roughly chop the tomatoes and garlic. Place in a food processor and blend together until finely chopped.
Add the remaining ingredients and blend with a splash of water until thick and smooth.

SWEET CORN WITH CHILLI BUTTER

Sweet corn smothered in chilli butter always keeps hunger pangs at bay.

SERVES 2

2 sweet corn kernels
1 tablespoon salted butter

½ teaspoon chilli flakes
Salt and black pepper

Simmer the sweet corn kernels in water for 10 minutes.
While the corn is cooking gently melt the butter in a small pan, stir in the chilli flakes and season to taste.
Drain the corn and pour the chilli butter over the top.

POTATO CAKES

Transform leftover mashed potato into a simple satisfying snack, smear with butter and spread with marmite, homemade jam or honey.

MAKES 6 CAKES

225g/8oz leftover mashed potato
3 heaped tablespoons plain flour
I tablespoon melted butter

1 small free-range egg, beaten
Pinch of salt
Butter to fry

Mix all the ingredients together until a dough forms.

Coat the dough with flour and cut into 6 portions. Coat your hands with flour and roll each portion into a ball, flatten into cakes approximately 1 cm/½ inch thick.

Fry the cakes in butter until golden brown on both sides. Spread with extra butter and enjoy while still hot.

CHOCOLATE ALERT

It's no wonder the Aztecs considered chocolate a food for the Gods – as it melts in the mouth it dispenses an instant feel good factor as endorphins and serotonin are released. Chocolates creamy sensual texture ensured its mythical status as a powerful love potion, and who would have thought cocoa could actually be good for you? It's now proven to reduce blood pressure, so chocolate really is good for the heart.

It pays to plan ahead for those chocolate alert moments. Here are a couple of choccy treats to have hidden in the back of the cupboard - healthy or decadent? Take your pick.

DARK CHOCOLATE DIPPED HONEY NUT BITES

You can almost convince yourself you are being virtuous when snacking on these nut packed choccy bites.

MAKES ABOUT 16
120ml/4 floz runny honey
2 tablespoons butter
Pinch of sea salt
350g/12oz mix of chopped walnuts, almonds, brasil and hazelnuts and
    sunflower seeds
A handful of chopped dates
75g/3oz good quality dark chocolate (preferably 70% cocoa solids)

Line a 18cm/7 inch square baking tray with baking parchment.

Melt the butter and honey in a small pan, stir well and gently simmer for 10 minutes or so, until the mixture has thickened to a toffee consistency. Add a pinch of salt.

Mix the nuts, seeds and dates together, add the honey toffee and stir together until well coated. Spoon the mixture into the prepared baking tray and spread evenly. Compact everything together with the back of a large spoon.

Place the baking tray in the fridge until the mixture has set hard enough to cut into bite size squares.

Melt the chocolate in a heat-proof bowl over a pan of simmering water. Dip the nutty squares into the melted chocolate and place on baking parchment until the chocolate has set. Store in an airtight container.

CHOCOLATE BROWNIES

Guess which option this is?

MAKES ABOUT 16
200g/7oz good quality dark chocolate (preferably 70% cocoa solids),
    broken into pieces
200g/7oz butter
3 large free-range eggs
250g/9oz caster sugar
1 teaspoon vanilla extract
110g/4oz plain flour, sifted
1 dessertspoon cocoa powder, sifted
150g/5oz chopped walnuts

Preheat the oven to 170°C/325°F/Gas mark 4 and line a 23cm/9inch square baking tray with baking parchment.

Melt the butter and chocolate in a heat-proof bowl over a pan of simmering water. Stir the chocolate and butter together to make a smooth chocolaty sauce. Set to one side and allow to cool a little.

Beat the eggs, caster sugar and vanilla extract together until light in colour and fluffy in texture. Gently fold in the cooled chocolate sauce, followed by the sifted flour and cocoa and finally stir in the chopped walnuts.

Spoon the mixture into the lined baking tray and bake in the preheated oven for 35–40 minutes. The brownies should be crunchy on the outside and squidgy in the middle. Allow to cool and cut into squares.

FEET UP IN FRONT OF YOUR FAVOURITE FILM

Treats to curl up on the sofa with.

STRAWBERRY ICE CREAM

It's always good to have a medicinal tub of homemade ice cream on stand by in the freezer, for those moments when you can devour it with a spoon guiltlessly straight from the tub.

450g/1lb hulled strawberries
1 tablespoon freshly squeezed lemon juice
3 tablespoons icing sugar
300ml/½ pint double cream
1 teaspoon vanilla extract or rosewater

Blend ¾ of the strawberries in a food processor with the lemon juice and icing sugar until smooth. Roughly chop the remaining strawberries.

Whip the cream with the vanilla extract until it has a floppy, lightly whipped texture.

Fold the strawberry puree and chopped strawberries into the cream, pour into a freezer proof plastic tub and place in the freezer.

When the ice cream is half frozen, break up the ice crystals with a fork and stir together. Repeat this process once more then allow the ice cream to freeze completely.

If you can wait, it is best to leave the ice cream out of the freezer for 15 minutes before scooping.

BUTTER AND MAPLE SYRUP POPCORN

So much more fun to make your own.

    3 tablespoons sunflower oil
    A good pinch of sea salt
    75g/3oz popcorn kernels
    2 tablespoons butter
    4 tablespoons maple syrup

Place the oil, salt and popcorn kernels in a large saucepan with a fitted lid. Heat the pan on the stove top until the corn starts to pop, shake the pan (don't be tempted to lift the lid at this stage) and continue to cook until the corn has stopped popping. Remove the pan from the stove and pour the popcorn into a large bowl.

   Melt the butter in a small pan, stir in the maple syrup and simmer together for a few minutes, stirring constantly. Pour the buttery maple sauce over the popcorn and toss together until well coated.

Bake away the blues

★ ★ ★

Feeling blue, what to do? Time to put on an apron and get baking! Dig out your favourite childhood recipes and enjoy making a mess. There is nothing quite like the ritual of baking for putting things in perspective – by the time those wonderful smells are wafting from the oven the blues will be a distant memory.

COMFORTING CAKES

A mouthful of sumptuous cake never fails to fill you with that warm fuzzy feeling. Plump up the cushions and sink into the sofa and relax with a large slice of your favourite.

COFFEE AND WALNUT CAKE

Memories of village hall cake bake sales and tea with granny flood back with the first bite of this buttercream filled coffee and walnut cake.

175g/6oz soft unsalted butter
175g/6oz caster sugar
3 medium free-range eggs
1 tablespoon strong espresso coffee
  or 2 teaspoons instant coffee
  in 1 tablespoon warm water
175g/6oz self raising flour, sifted
60g/2½oz walnuts, chopped

Butter cream icing
125g/4½oz soft unsalted butter
200g/7oz icing sugar
1 tablespoon strong espresso coffee
  or 2 teaspoon instant coffee
  dissolved in 1 tablespoon
  warm water
A handful of walnut halves to decorate

Preheat the oven to 190°C/375°F/gas mark 5 and line 2 x 20cm cake tins with greaseproof paper.

Beat the butter and sugar together until pale in colour and fluffy in texture.

Beat in the eggs individually (making sure each egg is well incorporated before adding the next) and stir in the coffee until well combined.

Fold in the sifted self-raising flour and the chopped walnuts and divide the mixture equally between the prepared cake tins.

Level the top of the cakes and place on the middle shelf of the preheated oven and bake for 25 minutes, at which point the cakes should spring back when lightly pressed in the middle.

When the tins are cool enough to touch, turn out the cakes on to a cake rack, carefully remove the greaseproof paper and allow the cakes to cool completely.

Meanwhile make the butter cream; cream the soft butter and icing sugar together until light and fluffy and beat in the coffee.

Spread one of the sponges with half the butter cream, pop the second sponge on top and cover the top with the remaining butter cream. Decorate with walnut halves artistically placed around the edge of the cake.

VICTORIA SPONGE

Victoria sponge is so versatile; add the grated zest of a lemon to the cake mixture, fill the cooked sponges with good quality lemon curd and top with lemon icing (made by mixing 150g/5oz icing sugar with a generous tablespoon of lemon juice) and hey presto lemon curd cake! Or for something more reminiscent of birthday parties past try an iced tray bake. Spoon the cake mixture into a lined oblong cake tin and bake until golden, top with icing sugar mixed with a little water and sprinkle with desiccated coconut, serve cut into generous squares.

VICTORIA SPONGE WITH JAM AND CREAM

This classic moist and buttery sponge oozing with jam and cream has to be top of the list.

225g/8oz soft butter
225g/8oz caster sugar
1 teaspoon vanilla extract
4 medium free-range eggs
225g/8oz self raising flour, sifted
Strawberry jam
300ml/½ pint double cream, whipped until thick
Icing sugar, to dust

Preheat the oven to 190°C/375°F/Gas mark 5 and line 2 x 20cm cake tins with greaseproof paper.

Cream the butter, sugar and vanilla extract together until the mixture is pale and fluffy. Beat in each egg individually (making sure each egg is well incorporated before adding the next) and fold in the sifted flour. Spoon the cake mixture into the lined tins and gently level the top with a knife.

Place the cakes on the middle shelf of the preheated oven and bake for 20–25 minutes, at which point the cakes should be golden brown and the tops spring back when lightly pressed in the middle. Allow the cakes to cool for a few minutes in the tins before carefully turning out onto a cake rack. Peel away the greaseproof paper and allow to cool completely.

Assemble the sponge; spread one cake with strawberry jam and cover with the whipped double cream. Place the remaining cake on top and gently press together. Dust the top of the cake with sifted icing sugar. Feeling better?

LEMON DRIZZLE CAKE

Everybody's favourite, a lovely light melt in the mouth sponge with a zesty sugary topping.

175g/6oz soft butter
175g/6oz caster sugar
3 medium free-rang eggs
175g/6oz self-raising flour, sifted
Juice and zest of a lemon

Sugar topping
50g/2oz caster sugar
Juice and zest of a large lemon

Preheat the oven to 180°C/350°F/Gas mark 4 and line a loaf tin (approx 23cm/9inches x 13cm/5 inches) with greaseproof paper.

Beat the butter and caster sugar together until pale in colour and light and fluffy in texture. Beat in the eggs one by one and gently fold in the flour, stir in the lemon zest and juice.

Spoon the mixture into the prepared loaf tin and place on the middle shelf of the preheated oven. Bake for 40–45 minutes until golden brown (the cake should spring back when lightly pressed in the middle and a toothpick inserted in the middle should come out clean).

To make the lemon drizzle topping, gently warm the caster sugar with the lemon juice and zest until the sugar has completely dissolved. While the cake is still warm, liberally prick the top with a fork or a toothpick and pour the prepared syrup evenly over the top.

Allow the syrup to soak into the cake before turning out and removing the greaseproof paper.

SPICED BANANA AND RAISIN BREAD
WITH VANILLA MASCARPONE TOPPING

This homely cinnamon and cardamom spiced banana bread is an excellent way to use up any over ripe bananas in the fruit bowl. If you prefer to keep things simple, forget the topping and spread the sliced cake with butter.

110g/4oz melted butter
150g/6oz soft brown sugar
2 medium free-range eggs, beaten
1 heaped teaspoon ground cinnamon
½ teaspoon ground cardamom
1 teaspoon vanilla extract
225g/8oz self-raising flour, sifted
4 very ripe mashed bananas
Large handful raisins
Large handful chopped walnuts

The topping
1 small tub of mascarpone cheese
1 heaped tablespoon icing sugar
½ teaspoon vanilla extract

Preheat the oven to 180°C/350°F/Gas mark 4 and line a loaf tin (approx 23cm/9inches x 13cm/5 inches) with greaseproof paper.

Beat the butter, sugar, eggs, spices and vanilla together until well combined.

Fold in the flour and add the mashed banana, raisins and walnuts.

Scoop the mixture into the lined loaf tin and place on the middle shelf of the preheated oven. Bake for 1 hour, when a toothpick inserted in the middle should come out clean.

Allow the tin to cool a little before turning out the banana bread onto a wire rack, carefully peel away the greaseproof paper and leave to cool.

Combine the topping ingredients together until smooth and spread over the top of the cake.

TEA TIME TREATS

A steaming mug of tea and a freshly baked teatime treat will soon lift the heart. Take your pick from biscuits, homemade bread and scones.

CHOCOLATE CHIP SHORTBREAD BISCUITS

These moreish buttery chocolaty biscuits are far too good to dunk!

If you prefer fruity shortbread biscuits, replace the chocolate with raisins or chopped dates. Chopped hazelnuts also make a good variation.

MAKES ABOUT 12 BISCUITS

175g/6oz plain flour
50g/2oz caster sugar
Pinch of salt
110g/4oz soft butter, cut into small cubes

50g/2oz good quality dark or milk
chocolate, cut into smallish chunks
Caster sugar for dusting

Preheat the oven to 180°C/350°F/Gas mark 4

Sift the flour and salt into a mixing bowl and stir in the caster sugar. Add the butter and lightly rub into the flour mixture until breadcrumbs form. Add the chocolate chunks and gently knead together until a dough forms.

Transfer the dough onto a lightly floured surface and roll out until about ½ cm/¼ inch thick. Cut into 5cm/2 inch rounds and place on a non-stick baking tray.

Bake on the middle shelf of the preheated oven for 15 minutes or so, when the biscuits should be a pale buttery colour.

Remove the shortbread from the oven and sprinkle with caster sugar while still warm.

PLUMP DEVONSHIRE SCONES

There is nothing quite like a warm scone topped with jam and spoonfuls of thick clotted cream. They are pretty good just simply spread with butter for that matter.

The trick to pillowy soft scones is to handle the mixture as little as possible.

Why not try adding a handful of chopped dried cherries or blueberries to the mixture before adding the milk and egg for something different.

MAKES ABOUT 12
225g/8oz self raising flour
½ teaspoon baking powder
Pinch of salt
75g/3oz soft butter, cut into small cubes
25g/1oz caster sugar
Optional handful of dried cherries or blueberries, roughly chopped
1 large free-range egg
75ml/2floz whole milk

Preheat the oven to 220°C/425°F/Gas mark 7

Sift the flour and baking powder into a mixing bowl, add the soft butter and rub together (using your finger tips only, palms are too hot) until breadcrumbs form.

Beat the egg and milk together (setting 1 dessertspoon to one side for later) and pour into the bowl; lightly combine together until a soft dough forms.

Roll out the dough on a floured surface, until 2.5cm/1inch thick, cut into 5cm/2 inch rounds, using a fluted cutter and place the scones on a non-stick baking tray.

Brush the top of the scones with the milk/egg mixture and bake for 10–15 minutes, until golden brown and well risen.

When the scones are cool enough to handle split in half and top with jam and cream.

WHOLEMEAL SODA BREAD

Homemade bread in a hurry, made without the complication of adding yeast and a blissful no need to knead method, creating a perfect foolproof loaf every time. It's essential to help yourself to a healthy thick slice while the bread is still warm.

You can use any wholemeal flour in this recipe – spelt or kamut make a more unusual loaf with a light nutty flavour.

MAKES 1 LARGE LOAF
225g/8oz wholemeal flour
225g/8oz plain white flour
1 heaped teaspoon bicarbonate of soda
½ teaspoon salt
25g/1oz soft butter, cut into cubes
50g/2oz rolled oats
400ml/14 floz buttermilk

Preheat the oven to 200°C/400°F/Gas mark 6

Sift the flour, bicarbonate of soda and salt into a mixing bowl, add the butter and rub into the mixture.

Stir in the oats (setting a tablespoon aside for later) and make a well in the middle. Pour in the buttermilk and quickly combine together using a palate knife, until a slightly sticky dough forms.

Turn the dough out onto a floured surface and shape into a 20cm/8 inch round flattish loaf. Place the loaf on a lightly floured non-stick baking tray and cut a deep cross shape in the top with a sharp knife.

Sprinkle the bread with the remaining oats and bake in the preheated oven for 30 minutes until golden brown. When the loaf is cooked it should make a hollow sound when tapped on the bottom.

Place on a wire rack and allow to cool a little before cutting.

Drinks to pick you up
and put you to bed

★ ★ ★

*E*verything seems a lot better after a steaming cuppa. Whether you prefer a strong builders brew or delicate Darjeeling, tea is full of antioxidants and catechins, that not only help to perk you up but also calm you down.

NURTURING DRINKS TO PUT YOU BACK ON TRACK

Liquid medicine in a cup.

SPICED LEMON AND GINGER

Fresh ginger works wonders on a queasy tummy and soothes a sore throat.

PER PERSON
1 cm/½ inch ginger root, peeled and grated
2 cloves
2 allspice berries
Water
Juice of ½ a lemon
1 heaped teaspoon honey

Place the grated ginger, cloves and allspice in a small pan. Add a generous mug of water and gently simmer for 5 minutes.
Place the lemon juice and honey in a mug and strain the ginger water on top.
Stir all the flavours together and allow to cool a little before drinking.

HOT TODDY

Sometimes a hot toddy and an early night is all you need to ward off a looming cold or help you sleep.

PER PERSON

1 heaped teaspoon honey	Boiling water
A generous measure of whiskey	1 cinnamon stick
Juice of ½ lemon	Slice of orange

Spoon the honey into a sturdy mug or heatproof glass, pour in the whiskey and lemon juice and top with boiling water. Stir the hot toddy with the cinnamon stick until the honey has dissolved.

Float the orange slice on top and leave the toddy to infuse with the cinnamon for a few minutes until it is cool enough to sip.

HOT MILKY DRINKS TO CALM THE BODY AND THE MIND

Soothing bedtime drinks to melt away the stress of the day.

SPICED VANILLA MILK

Perfect for those moments when you can't be bothered to cook.

PER PERSON
1 mug of full fat milk
1 small cinnamon stick
A good pinch ground cardamom and nutmeg
¼ teaspoon vanilla extract
Maple syrup or runny honey to taste

Place all the ingredients in a small milk pan (except for the maple syrup). Warm together until just before boiling point.

Pour the spiced milk into a mug (holding back the cinnamon stick) and stir in maple syrup to taste.

HOMEMADE HOT CHOCOLATE

Liquid comfort in a cup, add a pinch of chilli powder for a spicy kick with a Mexican twist.

PER PERSON
275ml/½ pint full fat milk
30g/1¼oz grated dark chocolate (preferably 70% cocoa solids)
Honey or brown sugar to taste

Warm the milk in a small milk pan and when the milk reaches boiling point, reduce the heat and whisk in the grated chocolate (and chilli). Sweeten with honey or brown sugar to taste.

WINTER WARMERS

Spicy, warming nectars to sip by the fireside.

BRANDY ALEXANDER

A luxurious, silky smooth cocktail to get the evening started.

SERVES 4
200ml/7floz brandy
200ml/7floz dark crème de cocoa
200ml/7floz single cream
Ice
Freshly grated nutmeg

Pour the brandy, dark crème de cocoa and single cream into a cocktail shaker, add a large handful of ice, cover and shake enthusiastically for a few minutes.

Pour the brandy Alexander into cocktail glasses and grate a sprinkling of nutmeg on top.

MULLED WINE

Why wait for Christmas?

If you are having a teetotal moment replace the wine with any red berry or grape juice.

SERVES 4
150ml/¼ pint water
2 cinnamon quills
10 cloves
A good grate of nutmeg
3 tablespoons brown sugar or honey
2 clementines, cut into quarters
1 unwaxed lemon, cut into quarters
1 bottle full bodied red wine
A good glug of port

Place the water, spices and sugar in a small saucepan. Add the clementines and lemon quarters (squeezing them with your hand as you do so) and warm everything together over a low heat until the sugar has dissolved. Bring the pan to the boil, cover with a lid, reduce the heat and gently simmer for 10 minutes.

Pour the wine and port into a medium pan and add the spice mixture. Gently warm together for 10 minutes or so, to allow the flavours to blend together (taking care not to boil the mulled wine or the alcohol will burn off).

Strain the mulled wine into heatproof glasses and serve while piping hot.

SPICED CIDER

Make bonfire night go with a bang with this gingery mulled cider.

Feel free to substitute cider with unsweetened apple juice if you prefer.

SERVES 4
1 litre /1¾ pints still dry cider
Thumb sized piece ginger root,
  peeled and sliced
8 cloves
2 star anise
6 cardamom pods, slit
1 cinnamon stick, plus 4 to serve
4 thick strips of orange peel
  (peeled with a vegetable peeler)
Honey to taste

Gently simmer all the ingredients together for 10 minutes, taking care to prevent the cider from boiling, as this will reduce the alcohol content.

Strain the spiced cider into heatproof glasses, add a cinnamon stick and sip while still hot.

INDEX OF RECIPES